CALIFORNIA'S INDIANS AND THE GOLD RUSH

by Clifford E. Trafze

Sierra Oaks Publishing Company
1989

Other Children's Books by Sierra Oaks Publishing Company:

A, B, C's The American Indian Way
Creation of a California Tribe: Grandfather's Maidu Indian Tales
Grandfather's Origin Story: The Navajo Indian Beginning
Grandfather's Story of Navajo Monsters
Grandmother Stories of the Northwest
A Trip to a Pow Wow
Where Indians Live: American Indian Houses

Copyright © 1989

Sierra Oaks Publishing Company
1370 Sierra Oaks Court
Newcastle, CA   95658-9791

ISBN: 0-940113-21-X

For my children, whose Wyandot ancestors participated in the Gold Rush, and for California's Indian children, whose people contributed to the growth and development of the Golden State.

The author extends special thanks to Professor James Rawls for his assistance.

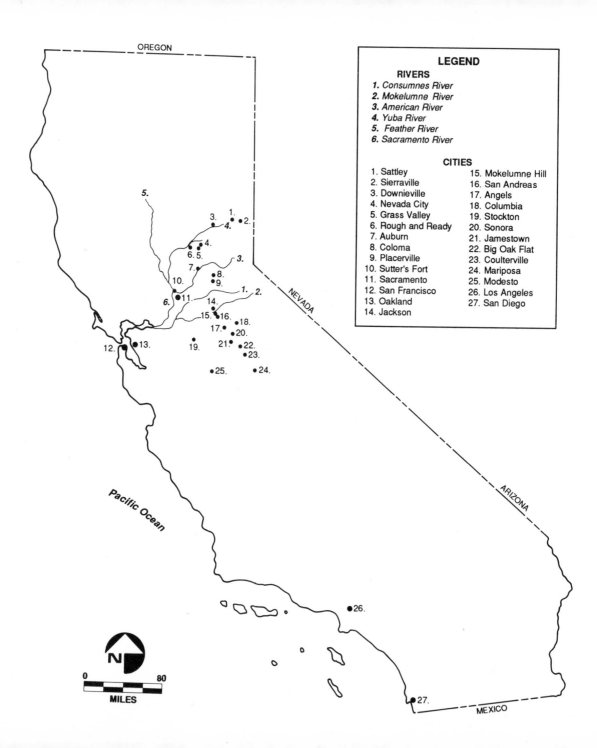

OREGON

LEGEND
RIVERS
1. Consumnes River
2. Mokelumne River
3. American River
4. Yuba River
5. Feather River
6. Sacramento River

CITIES
1. Sattley
2. Sierraville
3. Downieville
4. Nevada City
5. Grass Valley
6. Rough and Ready
7. Auburn
8. Coloma
9. Placerville
10. Sutter's Fort
11. Sacramento
12. San Francisco
13. Oakland
14. Jackson
15. Mokelumne Hill
16. San Andreas
17. Angels
18. Columbia
19. Stockton
20. Sonora
21. Jamestown
22. Big Oak Flat
23. Coulterville
24. Mariposa
25. Modesto
26. Los Angeles
27. San Diego

NEVADA

ARIZONA

Pacific Ocean

N

0   80
MILES

MEXICO

CALIFORNIA'S INDIANS AND THE GOLD RUSH

California Indians quarrying. Courtesy United States National Museum.

CALIFORNIA GOLD

GOLD! The word fires the imagination. It brings to mind riches beyond belief. Thoughts emerge of rough miners with mustaches and beards. People think back to a time when "sourdough" miners wandered over the rolling hills, rocky valleys, and pine-covered mountains of the Golden State. The tough miners of California's past searched the land over for paydirt.

Gold is very much a part of California's colorful past and the past of many people living within the state. Anglos, Hispanics, Chinese, and others participated in the California Gold Rush. California Indians were also struck by the gold fever. They played an important role in the early stages of California's mining frontier. The story of California's Indians and the gold begins with the exciting discovery of "color," as gold was called by the early miners, on January 24, 1848.

DISCOVERY OF THE GOLD

In May of 1847 an Indian scout led James Marshall and a group of men out of Sutter's Fort. The group included white men and Indians.

John A. Sutter. Courtesy California State Library.

James Marshall. Courtesy New York Public Library.

Together they started a journey in search of a good location to build a sawmill. The Indians and Marshall worked for the famous German Swiss, John A. Sutter. Marshall was a master carpenter, and Sutter had hired him to locate a mill site in the foothills of the Sierra Nevada Mountains of California.

White men in the Sacramento Valley needed lumber to satisfy the needs of increasing settlement and development in the area. Sutter planned to supply this lumber by building a sawmill. The Indian guide led Marshall up the American River into the foothills of the Sierra Nevada Mountains. Along the way they met Maidu Indians, the American Indian residents of the region. The Maidus and Marshall respected each other. They treated each other in a friendly manner as the small party made its way deeper into the foothills.

The Indian scout and Marshall traveled up the American River to a Maidu village called Koloma. Koloma is a Maidu Indian word which means "beautiful vale." The village of Koloma was located northeast of Sutter's Fort about 45 miles. The Indian scout and the carpenter surveyed the land around the Maidu village, a place they recorded as Coloma. Large evergreen trees dotted the landscape, and the clear waters of the American River rushed over a stony bed of round, smooth rocks. This was an ideal spot for a sawmill. Wagons filled with lumber or supplies could move easily from Sutter's Mill to Sutter's Fort.

Sutter's Fort, 1848. Courtesy New York Public Library.

Sutter's Fort with an Indian entering at the far right. From Revere, *A Tour of Duty in California*, 1849.

The Maidu Indians living at Coloma acted kindly toward Marshall. They did not prevent him from beginning work on the sawmill. Rather, the Indians helped with the work. Marshall hired Maidu men to clear the land and cut wood. He probably hired Maidu women to help Jenny Wimmer cook for everyone. Marshall's white assistants, Peter Wimmer and James Brown, learned how to speak some of the Maidu language. They worked side by side with the Indians, and they were impressed by the excellent job done by the Maidus. Brown and Wimmer had some of the Maidu men dig out a portion of the riverbed to make a "mill race." A mill race was created by digging out a channel so that water from the American River would rush through and move a large wooden wheel on the side of the sawmill. The raging water provided power for the saw which would cut huge trees into boards.

While the Indians dug the mill race, the first color or pieces of California gold were discovered. Marshall recalled that he found the gold on January 24, 1848. Some people, including college professors, have said that the Indians found the first gold. Indians led Marshall to Coloma and Indians dug the mill race. They probably found the first gold. In one story, a California Native American named "Indian Jim" found the first gold nugget. The nugget was larger than a nickle. "Indian Jim" showed it to white men working with the Indians. They showed it to Marshall, and the carpenter asked an Indian to bring him a tin pan. Marshall kneeled down along the banks of the American River and began washing the dirt. He found gold!

THE FIRST INDIAN MINERS

At first, Marshall claimed that he had found the first gold. Years later, Marshall admitted that "white and Indian" people found the first gold. Certainly many Indians were on hand that day in January when gold was discovered. The Indians at the Maidu village were present, as well as other Indians who had taken jobs at the mill. The discovery was to change the lives of all California Indians forever. This was particularly true for Indians living in the area of the California foothills. Soon after the workers discovered gold at Coloma, several Indians from many different tribes found work as miners. Many of them hired on with the Stockton Mining Company. Charles M. Weber, a rancher from Stockton who had once worked for Sutter, hired Indians to find the gold. Most of the Indians had already worked for Weber at his Stockton ranch.

Most of the California Indians who worked the placers during the first stages of the Gold Rush had worked on the *ranchos*. The owners of these ranches left their lands to seek fortunes in the gold fields. When they did, they took their Indian workers with them. This was true of Weber and

Sutter's Mill, Coloma, with Indians at the far right. From Taylor, *California Life*, 1858.

California Indian miners. From Bartlett, *Personal Narrative of Exploration*, 1854.

many miners. In the early months of 1848, Weber and his Indian cowboys traveled into the foothills. The party went to a beautiful mountainous spot called "Dry Diggings." This place is known today as Placerville, and about 1000 Indians worked with Weber to find the gold.

The Indians and Weber were soon joined by William Daylor. He was a rancher from the Sacramento Valley. Like Weber, Daylor also employed many Indians. Together, the two groups soon earned $50,000. However, the Indians received very little of this money. Weber and Daylor paid them in trade goods, including food, clothing, and blankets. The arrangement was beneficial to the mining company, and Weber recruited more Indians to work for him.

In the summer of 1848, Weber made a contract with José Jesus, a headman of the northern branch of the Valley Yokut Indians. Under the terms of the agreement, the Yokuts worked for meat, beans, sugar, coffee, clothing, and other supplies. Some of the Indians traveled to Placerville to learn how to pan for gold. Other Yokuts rode to the foothills farther south in present-day Calaveras and Stanislaus Counties. Soon after arriving, the Yokut Indians found gold on Wood's Creek and Carson's Creek. This began a new gold rush to what became known as the Southern Mines. The gold in this area was so rich that Weber soon moved his entire enterprise from Placerville to the Southern Mines.

Placerville, California. Courtesy California State Library.

California's Indians moved from ranches to the gold fields. From Forbes, *California*, 1839.

Indian miners working the placers. From *Hutchings' Illustrated California Magazine,* 1855.

Colonel Richard B. Mason, ex-officio governor of California, met Weber during a tour of the gold fields in the summer of 1848. The miner reported to the governor that two other white men were mining gold nearby. The other company employed five white men and a hundred Indians. At the end of one week, Weber said that the newcomers had cleared $10,000. Weber and the other mining companies were successful in large measure because of their Indian employees.

California Indians joined in the Gold Rush on a large scale. According to the *Monterey Californian,* there were 3000 Indians working in the mines in August, 1848. Another account estimated that by December, 1848, 4000 Indians worked the gold placers of California along with 2000 whites. During the same year, Colonel Richard Mason observed that over half of the miners in California were Indians. Most of the Indian miners worked for mining companies like that of Weber and Daylor. Other California Indians set out on their own to stake a claim.

HOW INDIANS MINED THE GOLD

Before the discovery of gold at Coloma, Indians of California had little knowledge of gold mining. Certainly, they had not exploited the gold reserves in California. Maidu, Miwok, Yokut, and other Indians had lived in the "Gold Country" for hundreds of years. Many of California's Indians had mined salt, obsidian, flint, crystals, turquoise, slate, and chalk. They probably knew about the gold, but they had not mined it. Many Indians lived within the area that became known as the "Mother Lode." This region was a huge area of land, extending 120 miles north to south in the mountains of the Sierra Nevada. Thousands of gold veins ran through the region. Some of the veins were 100 feet wide while others were up to two miles wide.

Years before the discovery of gold, the earth's crust lifted up high into the air. This uplifting caused the Sierra Nevada Mountains to form. When this occurred, molten gold ore flowed like rivers inside of the earth. The gold cooled and most of it remained hidden in the grey granite rock. Many years passed, and the surface of the earth changed. Wind and rain washed some of the gold down from the mountains. Gold flakes and nuggets lodged in the creeks and rivers of California. Pieces of gold often became mixed with the sand and mud of river beds and sandbars. Gold became lodged behind rocks or in pot holes. This gold is known in Spanish as *placer* gold. This became the common term used for the type of gold usually mined by California's Indians.

The Indians of California lived in the region of the "Mother Lode" long before the arrival of the Spanish, Russians, or Americans. Although they did not mine the gold, Indians likely knew about the colorful metal in

Sutter's Mill, 1849. Courtesy Huntington Library.

Shadowy figures of Indians in the Sierra Nevada Mountains. Courtesy, Yuma County Historical Society.

Sutter's Mill. Courtesy Huntington Library.

Long Tom. From *Harper's New Monthly Magazine*.

the streams. The California Indian economy was not based on precious metals. They did not believe in gathering wealth and keeping it from others. Rather, the Indians believed in communal welfare and in sharing their bounty. The Spanish, Russians, and Americans often found such ideas strange, because they did not understand the Indian way of life in California.

The Maidus at Coloma learned how to take the gold from the American River by panning it. This was a simple method of obtaining gold, but it was hard work. Another method of getting the gold was to use a "rocker." This was a long box that had no top, and it was set on rockers. It looked like an old baby's cradle. Indian miners set the rocker on a slope, and three people operated it. One person shoveled dirt into the hopper on the upper end of the rocker. Another person poured buckets of water over the dirt. The dirt moved down hill through the box. The third person rocked the device quickly. The dirt washed through the rocker. The "cleats" in the bottom of the rocker caught the gold and held it there.

By the end of 1849, Indians used a new device called the "long tom." The long tom was made from wood and was about 12 feet long. Indians placed the long tom where a stream of water could be run through it, driving the sand out and catching the particles of gold. The long tom did not move. It depended on the force of the water to move the mud. The Indian miners and others found that the long tom had a "great advantage over the popular cradle." It permitted "the speedy washing of larger quantities of earth." The long tom soon became the "sluice." This was a number of boxes fit together in a string. Sometimes a sluice was hundreds of feet long. Indians helped build dams, ditches, and wooden flumes that carried water to the long toms and sluices.

INDIAN CHILDREN AND THE GOLD RUSH

American Indian children in California participated in the Gold Rush. Girls and boys often lived with their parents and grandparents in the gold fields. Some of the children were born in the Sierra foothills where the gold was discovered. Other Indian children moved to the diggings with their families. The Indian boys and girls usually lived in houses built by their parents in a "traditional" fashion. The children helped their parents make homes from logs, sticks, grasses, and earth. Entire Indian families lived in these comfortable homes in the heart of the gold country.

Indian girls and boys spent their days in work and play. Young children laughed, ran, and played near the diggings. They had great fun playing near the edge of the swift streams and thick, green woods. Boys and girls climbed the huge rocks that lined the streams of the foothills. The younger and older children often spent their evenings learning from their

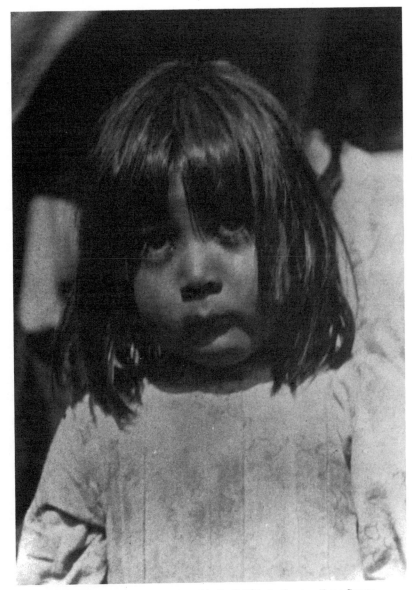

Indian children of all ages participated in the Gold Rush. Courtesy Yuma County
Historical Society.

mothers, fathers, aunts, uncles, and grandparents. This was particularly true in the winter months.

In the evenings the children listened to their elders. The old ones taught the young ones about the history of the people. For Indians, their history began at the time when the earth was first created. The children also learned about plants, animals, mountains, and rivers. These were special stories to the Indians, and the children were expected to pay close attention. Indian elders expected the children to learn their lessons and remember the stories. When the children were old enough, the elders asked the children to repeat the stories precisely as they had heard them. If the children did not repeat the story exactly, they were asked to listen carefully and learn it. The children would try again and again until they told the story correctly in every detail. In this way, the Indians educated the children. Just as important, this method of educating children enabled the Indians to keep the stories alive.

The older children were taught in the same way. Indian elders expected these children to be responsible. Children ten years and older had to help their parents. Some of their chores included gathering acorns, berries, and roots. Indian children also hunted game and fished as a way of helping their elders. Families relied upon their children to help build homes and cook meals. Older children also helped their parents dig for gold and pan the dirt. They learned how to help their families mine the

Interior of an Indian home. From Bartlett, *Personal Narrative of Explorations*, 1854.

Style of some California Indian homes. From Revere, *A Tour of Duty in California*, 1849.

Mothers taught children the traditions. Courtesy Lowie Museum.

color. The role of California's Indian children in the Gold Rush has been ignored too long. Their presence on the California gold frontier was important and should be recognized.

CULTURAL CHANGE AND INDIAN MINERS

When workers at Sutter's Mill first found gold, Maidu and Nissenan Indian families quickly joined the Gold Rush. Men, women, and children panned for gold using their native baskets and wooden bowls. Some of these Indians worked for Marshall. Other Indians worked for the many mining companies that began after the discovery of gold. Still other Indians worked for themselves, gathering the gold in cloth sacks and trading it for food, supplies, and manufactured goods. The discovery of gold caused many problems for the Indians. The primary problem was to answer this question: Should Indians dig for gold or not? Divisions arose within the Indian communities. Some of the Indians chose to participate in the mining frontiers and others did not. Entire families split over the issue.

The Indians who resisted the gold fever are called conservatives or traditionalists. These Indians feared that they would not be able to keep their cultures if they joined the gold rush. Often these Indians were elders who were rich in life's experience. They worried that the Indian people would become dependent on white trade goods. The Indian miners used their gold to purchase trade items. Trade between Indians and non-Indians worried the elders. Trade items--such as metal pots, pans, knives, fishhooks, axes, and shovels--would change the Indian way of life by making Indians dependent on items they could not produce for themselves. Rather than hunt meat and gather fruit and vegetables for a living, Indians would mine gold and live like white people. In the process they might forget how to live on their own, in the traditional manner. The elders talked about this problem, and they were greatly concerned.

As non-Indian miners invaded Indian lands, some native Californians fought the miners with bows, arrows, and guns. Colonel Mason felt that the Indians were justified in their anger toward the miners. He said that the "Indians are right in pressing their wish that the whites should not intrude on their lands." Still, the violence of whites and Indians led to more violence. Indians killed Captain William H. Warner while he was surveying a railroad route in the Sierra Nevada Mountains. Soon miners like Bayard Taylor worried "at the thought of an arrow sent out of the gloom around us." Such thoughts "made our backs feel uncomfortable as we stood before the fire."

California's Indians also had much to fear from the white miners. According to William McCollum, in his book, *California As I Saw It*, some white men hated all Indians. They hated Indians in California so much so

Indian girls wearing cloth dresses. Courtesy Yuma County Historical Society.

Indian women and children were not spared the violence. Courtesy Yuma County Historical Society.

that they "hunt them as they would wild beasts." Some whites would "leave a rich placer to wreak his vengeance on one of the race that he has learned to regard as his foe." These miners considered California's Indians to be "bad specimens of humanity" who should be hunted down and killed like wolves.

In March of 1850, a group of miners set out to exterminate the Indians living in the Napa Valley. The miners chased Indian workers from several ranches and killed at least seventeen men, women, and children. Similar problems arose near Auburn, California, where miners murdered twenty-five Maidu Indians. Such clashes hurt relations between all whites and Indians. Unfortunately, Indian children were victims of the fighting. They were innocent of any wrong doings but were harmed because of the fact that they were Indian children.

Despite the violence and the warnings of the elders, many Indians worked in the gold fields. In his book, *The Conflict between the California Indians and White Civilization*, S. F. Cook tells us about Indians as miners. He reported that "practically the entire native population of the Sierra foothills" panned for gold. This included all of the Indian people "from the Feather [River] to the Merced." The Indian participation in the Gold Rush would not be long lived. When California Indians began leaving the gold fields, they returned to their people or their former jobs on the ranches. When they returned to their own tribes, they patched up differences among tribal members.

California Indian culture changed as a result of the Gold Rush. The Indian miners who had moved away from their traditional homelands to the mines learned to buy things with their gold. Entire Indian families, including the children, relocated to the gold digging sites and enjoyed trading their precious metal for trade goods. Many of the Indians wanted to use their gold to buy trade goods.

With their gold, Indians bought foods such as meat, beans, flour, coffee, and sugar. They also purchased utensils and tools such as metal pots, pans, knives, axes, picks, and shovels. Blankets, beads, and broadcloth were also purchased by the Indian miners. California's Indians also used their gold to trade for strong rope, colorful handkerchiefs, and bright cloth for clothing. The Indians grew fond of these trade goods, and they learned to enjoy having such items. Having these things and learning to trade for them changed the Indians greatly.

INDIANS AND TRADERS

White traders set up commerce with Indians soon after the discovery of gold. By October of 1848, Colonel Mason and three other men established

Indians traded for cloth and chairs. Courtesy Southwest Museum.

a trading post on the American River near Sutter's Mill. The store was run by N. S. Bestor, a former Army clerk. He was one of many traders who sold goods to California's Indians. The Indian people were anxious to get such goods and were willing to pay high prices for manufactured items.

Indians bought many goods from white traders. In the early part of the Gold Rush, the traders were not always fair to Indians. The Indians living in the foothills of the Sierra Nevada Mountains still remember dealing with these traders. Their ancestors preserved these memories in stories passed down from generation to generation.

Other sources indicate that Indian stories of unfair treatment by traders are true. White miners left several written stories about traders cheating Indians. Sometimes problems between Indians and traders developed because of the different languages spoken by Indians and traders. The traders spoke English and Spanish. They usually did not speak Indian languages. The Indians spoke their own languages and some Spanish. Because they could not understand each other very well, problems in communication developed between the Indians and the traders.

Many Indians had never bought goods from traders until the Gold Rush. At first they did not understand how to trade. They did not read and were inexperienced shoppers, not knowing whether prices charged on goods were fair or inflated. As a result, some traders charged lower prices

Yokut Indian children visited traders with their parents.
Courtesy Southwest Museum.

Indian traditions changed with the Gold Rush. Courtesy Yuma County Historical Society.

to white miners and higher prices to Indians. The higher prices were commonly called "Indian Prices." For example, one of the Forty-Niners named James Carson said that he had seen traders charge Indians anywhere from $50 to $500 for colored handkerchiefs and a string of beads.

In 1848 and 1849 Indians often visited traders. William McCollum reported that two Indian miners "got their eyes" on "a pair of beaded moccasins, such as are sold at Niagara Falls." The white man selling the moccasins wanted an ounce of gold for the pair. When both Indians asked to buy the moccasins, the trader separated the pair. He sold each for an ounce of gold and doubled his profit. At the time, gold was worth $16 an ounce. In this case, the trader made $32 for the pair of moccasins.

Indians trading at stores usually set their sacks of gold or nuggets down and began gathering up items. They did this until the trader told them to stop. Traders sometimes sold Indians one pound of beads for one pound of gold. Traders sold blankets to Indians for gold weighing ten or twelve ounces. These were very high prices, much higher than what non-Indians paid for the same items. Soon the Indians learned about weighing their gold on scales. They began demanding that traders weigh Indian gold just as they did that of white miners.

As soon as the Indians learned about weighing gold, the traders found another way to cheat Indians. Instead of using a one ounce weight to measure gold, the traders started using a two ounce weight whenever an

Indian came in to trade. The traders made a new weight just to weigh Indian gold. It was a two ounce weight called a "Digger Ounce." How could the traders justify this kind of cheating, simply because the people they were cheating were Indians?

Some traders and miners did not like California's Indians because they lived in a different way. Some white people believed that the Indians were "inferior" because the Indians lived off the land. Most Indians dug wild roots as part of their food. For this reason, whites labeled California's Indians "Diggers." They used this term to belittle Indians, by making them seem less human than non-Indians. The traders and miners who cheated Indians believed it was acceptable to do so. They claimed that the Indians were "Diggers" and did not deserve to be treated equally with non-Indian people.

In his book, *An Excursion to California*, published in 1851, William Kelly stated that "no Christian man is bound to give full value to those infernal red-skins." He called California's Indians "vagabones" who could not handle money. He compared the Indians to mules and wolves. Such attitudes led traders to feel justified in charging outrageous prices. As a result, some traders earned between $10,000 and $20,000 each day! This gigantic profit may have encouraged the cheating traders to believe Indians were inferior. That way, they could continue to make large sums of money off Indians.

Sacramento's J Street was a major trading center for the northern mines. From Buck, *A Yankee Trader in the Gold Rush*, 1930.

Jamestown traders provided goods to Indians. Courtesy California State Library.

But while some miners agreed with Kelly's view of Indians, others did not. These other miners felt that it was wrong to cheat Indians. Believing that Indians were trustworthy and good people, many miners did not like it when traders cheated Indians. As the Indians learned more about trading, they discovered that some traders cheated them. When this happened, the Indians tried to put an end to the cheating without bloodshed.

INDIAN FORTY-NINERS

Most of the Indian miners who worked in the gold fields were native California Indians. However, some of the Indian miners came from other parts of the United States. They were Indian Forty-Niners who joined in the Gold Rush of 1849. When news of the gold discovery at Coloma and other places reached the outside world, a great gold fever swept across the world. People from far and wide moved to California. This was true of American Indians in the United States.

Indian Forty-Niners came to California in much the same manner as other Forty-Niners. Some came to California by ship. This was particularly true of Indians from the Pacific Northwest like Chinooks,

Some miners disliked all Indians, including children. Courtesy Yuma County Historical Society.

Walla Wallas, and Yakimas. Most of the Indian miners came to California by way of land, using routes such as the Santa Fe Trail, Gila Trail, and Oregon-California Trail. Indians living near the trails were affected by the migration of all of the "Argonauts." The Dakotas, Lakotas, Comanche, Kiowa, Apaches, Paiutes, Quechans, and others had to deal with the influx of thousands of gold seekers. Indians as well as whites used such trails, making their way west.

When word of the gold discovery reached the Wyandot Indians, the tribe was living in Kansas. The United States Army had recently removed them from Ohio and Michigan to Kansas. When the Indians learned of the Gold Rush in the early months of 1849, they formed a joint-stock company. Investors included Indians and whites, and they were much excited about the prospects of California gold. On May 31, 1849 the Wyandot Mining Company set out for the new Eldorado using the Oregon-California Trail.

Their journey was not without difficulties. All of the members of the party fell ill from cholera, but they were saved by a white doctor named E. B. Hand. The Wyandots also had problems with Lakota warriors who stole some of their horses. Four Wyandots chased the Lakotas and rode into a camp of three hundred Plains Indians. The Eastern Indians "marched boldly into the encampment, announced their national name Wyandot, took possession of their animals and marched off without even returning a

Forty-Niners passed through Quechan Indian lands in southern California.   Courtesy Yuma County Historical Society.

Many miners arrived in San Francisco, 1849. From Taylor, *California Life*, 1858.

Wyandot Indians crossed the Great Plains to California. Courtesy Huntington Library.

thanks." The Lakota were impressed by such bravery and did not pursue the Wyandots.

The Wyandots arrived at Fort Laramie, Wyoming, on June 20, 1849. They moved across the mountains and high deserts, finally crossing the Sierra Nevada Mountains before the heavy snows fell in the passes. By October the Wyandots were working their claims on the shores of Lake Lassen where they found thousands of dollars worth of gold. Their letters home to family and friends on the Wyandot Reserve encouraged others to make the long trip west. In May of 1850 a second party of Wyandot Indians arrived in California. They set up their enterprise on the Feather River near present-day Wyandotte, California, in Butte County. The Wyandots discovered the gold in this region and soon were joined by hundreds of other miners. Soon other towns emerged, including Oroville, the largest of the local communities.

Like the Wyandots, other American Indians moved to California during the Gold Rush. Some of them remained in the state to start a new life. Others returned home to territories and states outside of California.

INDIANS WERE GOOD WORKERS

In the Gold Rush accounts written by whites, the writers often say that Indians were good and loyal workers. Most of the Indian miners worked for mining companies. The Indians had been good ranch hands, and they were good miners. The Indians were hard workers, and many people remarked about this fact.

Henry I. Simpson reported in his book, *Three Weeks in the Gold Mines,* that before sunrise Indian miners were up working. He reported that one morning he ate a "hurried meal" before walking down to the gold diggings. Along the river "were some forty odd of them, mostly Indians." The Indians were in water waist high, washing mud and sand with the use of baskets and pans. Indian miners made about $1 each day, but they were often paid in food and cloth.

John Sinclair was an early miner who hired Indians. He employed about fifty Indian miners who worked the North Fork of the American River. Using woven willow baskets, the Indian miners gathered gold worth $16,000. The Indian miners made other people rich, including Antonio Maria Sunol. He had a large ranch in the San Francisco Bay area, but in 1848 left his ranch with thirty Ohlone Indians. The Ohlones panned for gold on the American River, making Sunol a wealthier man. The Ohlones

Levina Dale's Wyandot ancestors traveled to California with the Wyandot Mining
Company. Trafzer family photo.

Miners wrote numerous accounts of their adventures in California. Courtesy Sutro Library.

Miners working the placers by hand. Courtesy Yuma County Historical Society.

received food, clothing, and supplies in payment for their efforts. However, the Indians never received the large sums of money earned by Sunol.

Like many Indians in California, the Miwoks mined gold. One of their earliest adventures into the mining frontier came in 1848. Some Miwoks joined the Gold Rush as a result of their friendship with John M. Murphy. This white man was married to the daughter of a Miwok headman. When workers discovered gold at Coloma, Murphy used his relationship with the Miwoks to hire Indian miners.

The Miwoks dug gold for Murphy's company. They found color at a place called "Murphy's Camp" in Calaveras County. The Indians numbered about 600 men and an unknown number of women and children. In his book, *Three Years in California*, Walter Colton stated that Murphy made money off the labor of these Miwoks. In return, the Miwoks received "provisions and blankets." In addition, each day Murphy "knocks down two bullocks. . .to furnish them with meat."

William Ryan visited Murphy's Camp and was impressed by the Miwok workers. In his book, *Personal Adventures in Upper and Lower California*, Ryan reported that a Miwok miner once found a chunk of gold weighing five pounds. It was "a very fine specimen of the ore." Ryan wrote that the Miwok had picked the gold out of a large rock with a knife.

TOWNS IN INDIAN COUNTRY

Indians found other riches of equal or greater value of the nugget mined by the Miwok in all of the gold fields. The Indian miners panned for gold from the Yuba River in the north to Mariposa in the south. Wherever the miners found gold, towns sprung up. Sometimes these mining towns developed where only Indian villages had been. At first the towns were tent cities. If the gold proved to be a good strike, the tent towns became permanent. Miners and merchants bought lumber and built entire towns. Some of these towns still exist, and California's Indians helped built them.

Indians mined gold near the present-day towns of Grass Valley, Nevada City, Auburn, Placerville, Jackson, Columbia, Jamestown, Sonora, Angels Camp, and many others. These towns have a rich and colorful past, and Indians played a significant role in that past. When the miners moved into an area, they altered the land in a major way. They built towns and opened businesses. Trees were cut down for firewood and lumber. The miners brought horses, cattle, and mules to lands that had never known these animals. The humans and the animals changed the world around them. By moving large amounts of dirt, the miners caused soil erosion and polluted the water. The land which Indian peoples had occupied for centuries underwent profound changes. Indians assisted those responsible

Sacramento, 1852. From Taylor, *California Life*, 1858.

Miners arrived in Sacramento aboard ships. Courtesy California State Library.

Shasta, California, 1854. From Grabhorn, *A California Gold Rush Miscelleny*, 1934.

Sacramento, California, 1849. From Letts, *A Pictorial View of California*, 1853.

for this change. Whether they realized it or not, they were helping to alter the land forever.

The history of each of the gold towns includes that of the Indian miners. Most of the miners in these towns were men. Few white women lived in the mining towns. This was particularly true during the first stages of the Gold Rush. Most of the women living near the gold towns were Indian women. Like Indian men, they helped mine the precious mineral. In his narrative about the Gold Rush, L. M. Schaeffer provided an excellent description of Maidu Indians living near Grass Valley, California. He wrote that there were several Indian camps around the town.

One day, Maidu women, "nearly every one of whom had a 'papoose' strapped to her back," visited Schaeffer. The Indians were gathering onions and other roots while Schaeffer dug and washed dirt looking for gold. The miner started laughing at the Indians in a friendly manner, and the women and children returned the laughter. "Finally they went off," Schaeffer wrote, "and I could hear them laughing at the idea of a man working" in the water, sand, and mud of the gold fields.

Schaeffer showed great interest in the Indians and often visited the village of a leader named Wemah. The miner once attended a Maidu ceremony in which the Indians allowed him to enter their sacred ceremonial lodge called a Roundhouse. Schaeffer was always treated with respect. In turn, he treated the Indians with respect. He reported that the "majority of Indians about Grass Valley were friendly to the 'whites;' others were disposed for war."

Entire Indian families spent their days in the gold towns. Indian men, women, and children often worked the gold diggings as a team. When the gold was discovered in Auburn, Grass Valley, and Nevada City, local Maidu and Nissenan Indians joined the Gold Rush. They used metal shovels, woven baskets, and wooden bowls to mine the placers. Usually the mother, father, and older children dug mud and sand from a sandbar in a stream. The Indians took the mud to shore where members of the family-- including the children--washed the contents.

Panning gold was back-breaking labor. Still, members of Indian families washed the mud slowly until the heavier gold fell to the bottom of their basket, bowl, or pan. An Indian child would dip their pan into the water over 100 times and gently swirl the pan at least 500 times. They always held one side of the pan higher than the other. They did this for ten or fifteen minutes before searching the bottom of the pan for gold dust, flakes, and nuggets. The children would pick out the gold while others brought in another load of mud to wash.

California's Indians lived near the new gold mining towns. They traded in the local stores, but they were not always welcome in all of the businesses. When the Indians miners left the gold fields, they usually did

Miners working with early machinery. Courtesy Yuma County Historical Society.

Weaverville, California. Courtesy California State Library.

San Francisco during Gold Rush. From Buck, *A Yankee Trader in the Gold Rush*, 1930.

Indians found jobs in cities like San Francisco. Courtesy Huntington Library.

not remain in the new towns. Instead, they returned to the ranches to work as cowboys. Some of them moved to San Francisco, San Jose, Oakland, San Diego, Sacramento, Los Angeles, or other large towns. There, they took wage-earning jobs. Many white people had left these cities to seek their fortune in the gold mines. When this happened, former Indian miners who had left the mines took the jobs available in the cities.

Most of the Indians in California simply returned to their own people. Often they lived far enough away from the gold towns to avoid trouble. Still, they lived close enough to sell food to the miners. Indians were excellent hunters, and they knew what foods to gather. The Indians took the bounty from the earth--venison, rabbit, raccoon, bear, acorns, blackberries, and roots--and they traded this food for items they wanted. California's Indians sold numerous kinds of foods in the gold mining towns. They were well paid for this food.

DECLINE OF THE INDIAN MINERS

By the early months of 1850, the Indian miners began to fade from the gold fields. The placer deposits had been well worked by this time, and there was far less placer gold to be found. Mining companies had become involved in the Gold Rush and had started to use new technology. While

Forty-Niners invading Indian lands. Courtesy California State Library.

New modes of transportation, 1849. Courtesy Yuma County Historical Society

companies started quartz mining and hydraulic mining, Indians were left with few areas to mine with their pans, rockers, and long toms. These are some of the reasons for the decline of Indian miners after 1850, but they are not the most important.

The primary reason for the decline of Indian miners was attitudes of new miners coming into California. Some of the Forty-Niners who moved into California brought with them a hatred of Indians. Some of them had known Indians in other parts of the country. Others had only heard negative things about Indians. Miners did not like California's Indians because they felt that it was not right to use Indians as laborers. That is, these miners felt that it was unfair for miners like Weber, Sunol, and Daylor to employ Indians. This gave the first miners an unfair labor advantage.

New miners from other regions of the country often protested against the use of Indian miners. Pierson B. Reading and sixty Indian miners had been working the placers along the Trinity River when some men from Oregon told Reading to get rid of the Indian workers. Reading reported that "parties came in from Oregon who at once protested against my Indian labor." To avoid trouble, Reading left the diggings on the Trinity. His experience was just the beginning.

The first trouble between the Forty-Niners and the California Indians came from Oregon miners. These were men who had learned to hate

Indians on their own frontiers. Many of them had little experience dealing with Indians, but they all knew of the Indian troubles in their territory. A few years before, a small band of Cayuse Indians killed the Reverend Marcus Whitman, Narcissa Whitman, and a few others at the Whitman Mission. An Indian war had resulted, but the Oregon Volunteers had not defeated the Cayuses. Instead, the Palouse Indians defeated the Oregon soldiers.

In the end, the people of Oregon hanged a few Cayuse Indian men. Still, many whites in Oregon hated Indians--all Indians. A terrible event occurred on the American River in March of 1849. A group of men from Oregon attacked a Maidu-Nissenan village and injured some of the Indian women. When the Maidu men tried to prevent this violence, the Oregon miners shot some of the men. Not long afterwards, some Maidu warriors attacked a group of Oregon miners and killed five of them.

The Oregon miners banded together into an army. They attacked some Indians on Weber's Creek and killed over twelve of them. The miners took several Indian prisoners and held them hostage. Some of these Indians were employees of James Marshall, and he was very upset with the entire action. The Oregon miners took eight of the Indian miners captured on Weber's Creek to Coloma. The Oregon miners told the Indians to join the other miners then working on the banks of the American River.

New machine to wash gold. Courtesy Yale University Library.

New methods and technologies were introduced. Courtesy New York Public Library.

Miners from Oregon often hated Indians. Sketch of Yreka, California. From Buck, *A Yankee Trader in the Gold Rush*, 1930.

When the Indian miners turned to walk down to the stream, the Oregon miners opened fire on them.

According to George Parsons in his book, *The Life and Adventures of James W. Marshall*, "there was not the shadow of justification for the atrocious deed." Marshall and others believed that the Oregon miners had unjustly accused these particular Indians of killings that they had not committed. When Marshall tried to stand up and defend the Indians, the Oregon men threatened his life. The cold-blooded murder of Indian miners at Coloma had a powerful effect on all Indian miners. Similar violence arose throughout northern California. Bayard Taylor reported in his book, *Eldorado*, that a band of California Indians discovered the gold at Volcano, California, near Indian Grinding Rock State Historical Park.

When news reached other miners of the gold discovery, they moved into the area. The California Indians "made room for them at once, and proposed that they should work peaceably together." All went well until a miner lost his pick and claimed that Indians stole it. A chief declared he would see if any of his people had taken the pick. When he ran off to see, "one of the whites raised his rifle and shot him." The Indians and whites armed themselves. The Indians moved into the mountains, leaving the gold fields. The whites worried about a possible attack.

Events such as that at Coloma and Volcano increased after 1850. The violence against Indian miners led the California Indians to give up the mining frontier. Some of the Indian miners remained in the foothills and mountains to find pay dirt. Most of them returned to their former homes to live in a rapidly-changing world. Some of them returned to the ranches, while others moved to areas near their old homes away from the hustle and bustle of the gold towns.

IMPORTANCE OF THE INDIAN MINERS

During the early stages of the California Gold Rush, American Indians were important in the mining frontier. The participation of men, women, and children of the various Indian nations was widespread. Today, the Indian contribution to the Gold Rush is not generally recognized. It was important, particularly during the early stages of the period. Indian men, women, and children provided the first large labor force on the California mining frontier. They were excellent workers who gave their time, energy, and abilities to make the Gold Rush successful.

California's Indians were on hand when the gold was first discovered at Coloma. Some historians believe that Indians found the first color on the American River. Certainly Indians made the first strikes in other parts of California. With the gold they earned, the Indian miners

James W. Marshall. Courtesy California State Library.

California Indian miners punishing a fellow miner. From Gerstaecker, *Scenes de la Vie Californienne*, 1859.

bought many items from the traders. The gold they spent helped stimulate the economy of California and enrich the merchants. Indians gave of themselves and their land after the gold discoveries. Throughout California new people arrived and settled on Indian lands. Miners, merchants, cobblers, bakers, and butchers built their homes and businesses on Indian lands.

Miners built towns on Indian lands. The newcomers claimed the land, forests, rivers, and minerals for themselves. The Indian land disappeared with the mining frontier, and their environment changed significantly. The newcomers took over Indian country and brought new laws to California. Some of the settlers recognized Indian rights but others did not. Some settlers hated Indians just because they were Indians who lived and thought differently from white people. Troubles arose near Coloma, and white miners pushed Indian miners from the gold fields. Soon the Indian miners decided to leave the mining frontiers and find a new life separated from the white people.

The Indians in California did not fade away and disappear. They made a living as best as they could. They survived a great deal of cultural change. California's Indians continue to contribute to the state. They have not forgotten their past in the Gold Rush but others have. Too often, the American Indian contribution to the growth and development of the Golden

State is forgotten. The importance of California's Indians to the Gold Rush, too long overlooked, was indeed great.